best
easy
dayhikes
Yellowstone

Bill Schneider

*Published in Cooperation
with Trails Illustrated Maps*

FALCON®
HELENA, MONTANA

©1997 by Falcon® Publishing, Inc.,
Helena, Montana.

Printed in Canada.
10 9 8 7 6 5 4 3 2

Cover photo by Michael S. Sample

Library of Congress Cataloging-in Publication Data
Schneider, Bill
    Best easy day hikes, Yellowstone / Bill Schneider.
        p.   cm.
    "Published in cooperation with Trails Illustrated Maps."
    ISBN 1-56044-574-2 (pbk.)
1. Hiking—Yellowstone National Park—Guidebooks. 2. Backpacking—Yellowstone National Park—Guidebooks. 3. Yellowstone National Park—Guidebooks. I. Title.
GV199.42.Y45S33   1997
796.51'09787'52—dc21   97-13475
                                                                          CIP

CAUTION

Outdoor recreational activities are by their very nature potentially hazardous. All participants in such activities must assume the responsibility for their own actions and safety. The information contained in this guidebook cannot replace sound judgment and good decision-making skills, which help reduce the risk exposure, nor does the scope of this book allow for disclosure of all the potential hazards and risks involved in such activities. Learn as much as possible about the outdoor recreational activities in which you participate, prepare for the unexpected, and be cautious. The reward will be a safer and more enjoyable experience.

 Text pages printed on recycled paper.

Contents

The Hikes

> **Note:** *The hikes are generally located on the Yellowstone National Park map on page vi.*

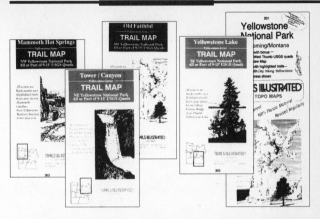

ALWAYS TAKE A GOOD MAP

The maps in this book are small sections of excellent topographic maps published by Trails Illustrated. The small size of pages in any guidebook prevent the inclusion of the type of map you really need to safely and thoroughly enjoy your walk in the wilderness. After surveying the line-up of maps available for Yellowstone, the author used Trails Illustrated maps and recommends that other hikers also use these handy, waterproof, tearproof and easy—to-read maps. Trails Illustrated has maps for many national parks, but in Yellowstone (one of our largest national parks), Trails Illustrated has split the park into four regions and published a map for each. This creates a large scale and the map is even easier to use and read. You can, however, also buy a Trails Illustrated map that covers the entire park.

Here is a list of the titles and coverage of the five maps available:

> *Mammoth Hot Springs (northwest section)*
> *Tower/Canyon (northeast section)*
> *Old Faithful (southwest section)*
> *Lake (southeast section)*
> *Yellowstone (the entire park)*

> *You can buy Trails Illustrated maps at park visitor centers*
> *or you can order them directly from Falcon*
> *by calling 1-800-582-2665.*

Yellowstone National Park

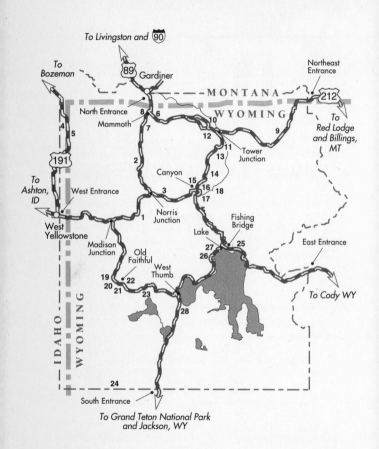

Introduction

What's a "best easy" hike?

While researching and writing a much larger book on Yellowstone National Park called *Hiking Yellowstone*, I had frequent discussions with rangers on what kind of information hikers most requested. I also had the same discussions with many hikers out on the trails.

It seems that there are at least these two general types of visitors—those who really want to spend several days experiencing the depth of the Yellowstone backcountry and those who only have a day or two and would like a choice sampling of the special features of Yellowstone. This book is for the second group.

Hiking Yellowstone covers almost every section of trail in the park, including those that are neither best nor easy.

Best Easy Day Hikes includes only short, less strenuous hikes that are my recommendations for the nicest day hikes in the park.

These hikes vary in length but most are short. With a few exceptions, none have seriously big hills. All hikes are on easy-to-follow trails with no off-trail sections. It's also easy to get to the trailhead of all hikes in this book, and you can get there with any two-wheel-drive vehicle.

Some of the hikes in this book might not seem easy to some hikers but will be easy to others. To help you decide, I've ranked the hikes from easiest to hardest. Please keep in mind that short does not always equal easy. Other factors such as elevation gain and trail conditions have to be considered.

I hope you thoroughly enjoy your "best easy" hiking experiences in America's first national park. —*Bill Schneider*

Preserving Yellowstone

The Yellowstone Association is a non-profit organization founded in 1933 to assist with educational, historical, and scientific programs for the benefit of Yellowstone National Park and its visitors. Through the years the Association has raised millions of dollars to help preserve Yellowstone and supplement the park's educational programs.

The Association operates bookstores in all park visitor centers and information stations with the proceeds from sales of books, maps, and videos going to fund interpretive programs and exhibits for visitors as well as for research projects and equipment. The Association also sponsors the Yellowstone Institute, an in-depth educational program for the pubic.

You can help preserve the park by becoming a member of The Yellowstone Association. Membership benefits include a newsletter, a subscription to the park newspaper, a discounton books, maps, and videos, and a discount on Yellowstone Institute tuition. All memberships or donations are tax-deductible.

To become a member or get more information on The Yellowstone Association, write The Yellowstone Association, P.O. Box 117, Yellowstone National Park, WY 82190 or call (307) 344-2296. To order books, maps, or videos call (307) 344-2293 or stop at any visitor center.

Ranking The Hikes

The following list ranks the hikes in this book from easiest to hardest.

Easiest

Boiling River
Natural Bridge
Artists Paintpots
Upper Geyser Basin
Lost Lake
Trout Lake
Tower Fall
Canyon Rim South
Canyon Rim North
Fairy Falls
Mystic Falls
Riddle Lake
Storm Point
Ribbon Lake
Sentinel Meadows
Bacon Rind Creek
Cascade Lake
Fan Creek
Beula Lake
Lone Star Geyser
Yellowstone Picnic Area
Ice Lake
Grizzly Lake
Hellroaring Creek
Beaver Ponds
Mount Washburn
Elephant Back Mountain

Hardest Bunsen Peak

Leave No Trace

Going into a national park such as Yellowstone is like visiting a famous museum. You obviously do not want to leave your mark on an art treasure in the museum. If everybody going through the museum left one little mark, the piece of art would be quickly destroyed—and of what value is a big building full of trashed art? The same goes for a pristine wilderness such as Yellowstone, which is as magnificent as any masterpiece by any artist. If we all left just one little mark on the landscape, the wilderness would soon be despoiled.

A wilderness can accommodate human use as long as everybody behaves. But a few thoughtless or uninformed visitors can ruin it for everybody. All hikers have a responsibility to know and follow the principles of leave no trace. An important source of these principles can be found in the book *Leave No Trace*. (Ordering information in the back of this book.)

Three Falcon Principles of Leave No Trace

- *Leave with everything you brought in.*
- *Leave no sign of your visit*
- *Leave the landscape as you found it.*

The wilderness is shrinking, and the number of users is mushrooming. More and more hiking areas show unsightly signs of heavy use.

Consequently a new code of ethics is growing out of the necessity of coping with the unending waves of people who want a perfect wilderness experience. Today we all must leave no clues that we have gone before. Canoeists can look behind the canoe

4

and see no trace of their passing. Hikers should have the same goal. Enjoy the wildness but leave no trace of your visit.

Most of us know better than to litter—in or out of the wilderness. Be sure you leave nothing, regardless of how small it is, along the trail or at the campsite. This means you should pack out everything, including orange peels, flip tops, cigarette butts, and gum wrappers. Also pick up any trash that others leave behind.

Follow the main trail. Avoid cutting switchbacks and walking on vegetation beside the trail.

Don't pick up "souvenirs," such as rocks, antlers, or wildflowers. The next person wants to see them, too, and collecting such souvenirs violates park regulations.

Carry a lightweight trowel to bury human waste 6-8 inches deep and pack out used toilet paper. Keep human waste at least 300 feet from any water source.

Finally, and perhaps most importantly, follow the pack-in/pack-out rule. If you carry something into the backcountry, consume it or carry it out.

Leave no trace—and put your ear to the ground in the wilderness and listen carefully. Thousands of people coming behind you are thanking you for your courtesy and good sense.

Types of Hikes

Loop: Starts and finishes at the same trailhead, with no (or very little) retracing of your steps.

Shuttle: A point-to-point trip that requires two vehicles (one left at the other end of the trail or a prearranged pick at a designated time and place.

Out-and-back: Traveling to a specific destination, then retracing your steps back to the trailhead

---

Northwest Region

1
ARTISTS PAINTPOTS

Type of hike: Out-and-back.
Total distance: 1.2 miles or 1.9 kilometers (round-trip).
Elevation gain: Minimal.
Maps: Trails Illustrated; Mammoth Hot Springs and Norris Junction USGS Quads.
Starting point: Artists Paintpot Trailhead.
Finding the trailhead: Drive south from the Norris Junction for 3.9 miles or 8.9 miles north of the Madison Junction on the Norris-Madison section of the Grand Loop Road and park at the Artists Paintpot pullout on the east side of the road at the south end of the Gibbon Meadows.

The hike: This short hike skirts the south edge of massive Gibbon Meadows and stays in the unburned lodgepole all the way. The trail is partly boardwalk and the rest is double wide, flat, and easy. Since elk commonly use Gibbon Meadows, you might see some on the way to the paintpots. However you probably won't see many people. Even though this trail goes to several interesting thermal features, it doesn't

Artists Paintpots

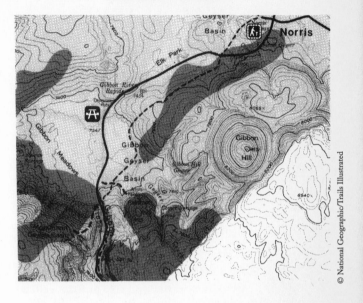

get nearly the use as trails in geyser basins around Old Faithful.

At the end of the hike on the slopes of Paintpot Hill, the trail makes a convenient little loop that provides good views of the major thermal features, primarily colorful paintpot formations (which early explorers thought resembled an artist's palette) as well as hot pools and steam vents. To protect both yourself and these fragile natural features, stay on the designated trail.

2

GRIZZLY LAKE

Type of hike: Out-and-back.
Total distance: 3.6 miles or 5.8 kilometers (round-trip).
Elevation gain: 400 feet.
Maps: Trails Illustrated; Mammoth Hot Springs, Obsidian Cliff, and Mount Holmes USGS Quads.
Starting point: Grizzly Lake Trailhead (1K8).
Finding the trailhead: Drive south 14.4 miles from Mammoth or 6.6 miles north of Norris on the Mammoth-Norris section of the Grand Loop Road and park at the trailhead, a pullout on the west side of the road.

The hike: The trail starts out nice and flat as it crosses Obsidian Creek on a footbridge and goes through a large meadow just south of Beaver Lake. At the west side of the meadow, the trail starts switchbacking up the side of the ridge. Also at this point, you may see a sign for the Howard Eaton Trail going from here to Mammoth; but that trail has been abandoned by the NPS.

The Grizzly Lake Trail stays on top of the ridge for a quarter mile or more before switchbacking down the other side to the north end of the lake. When you reach the 136-acre lake, the trail follows the shoreline for about 100 yards before reaching the outlet of the lake. If you're staying overnight, you have to carefully cross the outlet on a logjam to reach the campsites along Straight Creek below the lake.

Grizzly Lake

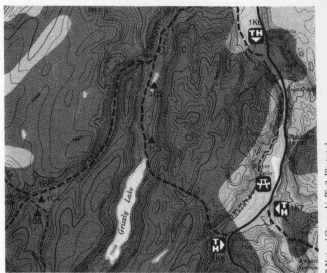

© National Geographic/Trails Illustrated

The trail is in great shape all the way. It winds through a burned forest the entire distance, except the large meadow at the trailhead and a few small meadows on top of the ridge. Grizzly Lake is a beautiful mountain lake tucked between two forested ridges, but it has been in the path of several forest fires, most recently the fires of 1988.

3
ICE LAKE

Type of hike: Loop.
Total distance: 4.5 miles or 7.2 kilometers.
Elevation gain: Minimal.
Maps: Trails Illustrated; Mammoth Hot Springs, Norris Junction, and Crystal Falls USGS Quads.
Starting point: Ice Lake Trailhead (4K2).
Finding the trailhead: Drive 3.5 miles east from Norris Junction or 8.5 miles east from Canyon and park at the Ice Lake Trailhead and parking area on the north side of the road.

Key points:

0.3 (0.5)   Spur trail to backcountry campsite 4D3.
0.5 (0.8)   Ice Lake.
0.6 (0.9)   Junction with Howard Eaton Trail.
0.8 (1.3)   Backcountry campsite 4D1.
1.5 (2.4)   Backcountry campsite 4D2.
2.3 (3.7)   Junction with Little Gibbon Falls/Wolf Lake Trail.
3.4 (5.5)   Little Gibbon Falls.
4.0 (6.4)   Norris-Canyon Road.
4.5 (7.2)   Ice Lake Trailhead.

The hike: The trail to Ice Lake gets fairly heavy traffic, but most hikers go out and back to the lake. Few hikers turn this into one of the few easy loop trips in the park, as described here. In addition to making a nice day hike, Ice

10

Lake provides a pleasant destination for an easy overnighter.

Ice Lake is fairly large and deep, and the lodgepole forest grows to the lakeshore. The fires of 1988 burned much of the landscape around the lake.

The first part of trail to Ice Lake is good enough for wheelchairs but only up to backcountry campsite 4D3. Beyond this point, the trail becomes a normal backcountry single track. It traverses the west end of the lake and joins the Howard Eaton Trail just after rounding the end of the lake.

Ice Lake

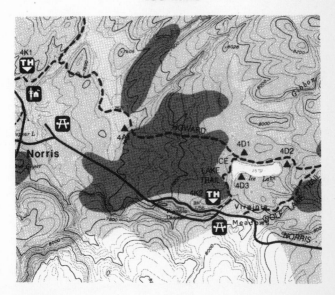

© National Geographic/Trails Illustrated

Turn right (east) at this junction and follow the north shore of the lake, going by 4D1 shortly after the junction. You pass the spur trail to 4D2 at the east end of the lake and ford the Gibbon River shortly thereafter. In summer this river could be described as a creek, and you'll have no problem fording it. After the ford, the trail continues east for another 0.7 mile to the junction with the Little Gibbon Falls Trail (called Wolf Lake Trail on some maps).

Turn right (south) at this junction and go another mile or so to 25-foot Little Gibbon Falls, which actually resembles the larger Gibbon Falls downstream along the Norris-Madison section of the Grand Loop Road. From the falls the trail drops into spacious Virginia Meadows along the Gibbon River until you reach the highway.

The trail is in good shape and stays in a mostly burned lodgepole forest much of the way, including all around the lake. The trail gets a little rougher on the last leg of the trip by Little Gibbon Falls, but it's still distinct with the exception of one spot near the highway where it disappears for about 100 yards in the lush meadow along the river. An orange marker on the other side of the meadow marks the route.

When you reach the highway, you have to walk less than a half mile along the paved road back to your vehicle.

Options: Hikers can hike out and back to Ice Lake or Little Gibbon Falls. This hike can also be an easy overnighter.

BACON RIND CREEK

Type of hike: Out-and-back.
Total distance: 4 miles or 6.4 kilometers (round-trip).
Elevation gain: Minimal.
Maps: Trails Illustrated; Mammoth Hot Springs and Divide Lake USGS Quads.
Starting point: Bacon Rind Trailhead (WK4).
Finding the trailhead: Drive south from Belgrade or north from West Yellowstone on U.S. Highway 191 and turn west on the Bacon Rind Road between mileposts 22 and 23 and follow the gravel road about a half mile to the trailhead.

The hike: This trail has the distinction of being the only trail heading west from the Gallatin Valley in the park. After the park boundary (at the 2-mile mark), the trail keeps going up into the Lee Metcalf Wilderness in the Gallatin National Forest. However, the trail gets faint and marshy as you near the park boundary. The map may show the trail crossing Bacon Rind Creek before the park boundary, but it stays on the north side of the stream.

This is a flat, easy trail along the bottomlands of Bacon Rind Creek. The stream contains a healthy population of rainbow trout, and willow thickets along the creek provide hiding places for moose and grizzly bears. If you plan to fish (catch-and-release only), be sure to get a park fishing permit.

The trail goes along the north side of the meandering stream as it winds its way through a beautiful mountain meadow with a strange (almost manmade-like) square-shaped hill in the middle of it. The trail crosses marshy Migration Creek just before reaching the park boundary, so this might be a good place to take a break before returning to the trailhead.

Bacon Rind Creek, Fan Creek

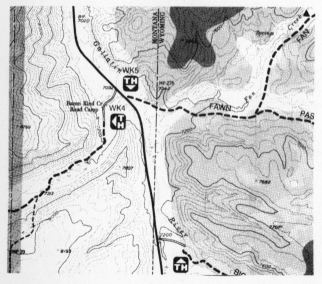

© National Geographic/Trails Illustrated

5
FAN CREEK

Type of hike: Out-and-back.
Total distance: 5-10 miles (round-trip).
Elevation gain: 430 feet.
Maps: Trails Illustrated; Mammoth Hot Springs, Divide Lake, and Quadrant Mountain USGS Quads.
Starting point: Fawn Pass Trailhead (WK5).
Finding the trailhead: Drive south from Belgrade or north from West Yellowstone on U.S. 191 to just south of milepost 22.

Key points:
1.4 (2.2) Fawn Pass Trail junction.
2.7 (4.3) WC2.
3.0 (4.8) Fan Creek Ford.
5.5 (8.8) Confluence of North and East forks of Fan Creek.

The hike: After hiking this trail, you could be easily convinced that Fan Creek is a shortened version of the original name, "Fantastic Creek." Although Fan Creek gets moderate to heavy use from trail riders taking long loop trips over to Gardner's Hole and back over Fawn Pass, the area is lightly used by hikers, but not because it isn't worthy of more attention. On the contrary, it's one of the most beautiful mountain valleys in the park.

The terrain doesn't completely open up until after the

Fawn Pass Trail junction where you turn left (northeast). You can go as far as 5.5 miles where the East Fork and the North Fork merge or you can go any lesser distance. At the 3-mile mark, you have to ford Fan Creek, but the crossing is usually less than knee-deep and easy in August.

If you're looking for an easy day hike possibly combined with some stream fishing, Fan Creek would be an excellent choice. There are no big hills, and the trail is in terrific shape the entire way. You might want to go early or stay late to watch elk, which are quite abundant in the area.

Options: If you want an easy overnighter, you can stay at WC2, a delightful campsite. It's a short backpacking trip (only 2.7 miles one way on a nearly level trail), but for beginning backpackers this could be just right.

6
BOILING RIVER⌖

Type of hike: Out-and-back.
Total distance: 1 mile or 1.6 kilometers (round-trip).
Elevation gain: Minimal.
Maps: Trails Illustrated; Mammoth Hot Springs and Gardiner USGS Quads.
Starting point: Boiling River Trailhead.
Finding the trailhead: Drive 2 miles north from Mammoth on the Mammoth-Gardiner section of the Grand Loop Road and turn into the Boiling River parking lot on either the north or south side of the road. The trail starts on the north side of the road.

The hike: Until the mid-1980s, the Boiling River was mostly a social hot tub for locals and park employees. Since then the National Park Service has made it an official trail and swimming hole.

The Boiling River is created by a massive hot spring discharge 2 feet deep and 6 feet wide (probably from the Mammoth Hot Springs) flowing into the Gardner River. The river has never been known to "boil," but it does get comfortably warm, and people have been soaking in this hot water for decades. Early promoters touted it as the only place you could catch a trout and boil it on the hook.

Now, the NPS has constructed a nice trail along the banks of the Gardner River to the hot spring, and it has become a very popular, short day hike. On a hot summer afternoon, expect to see dozens of people at the hot spring. The trail is easy and flat all the way.

Because of the extreme popularity of this hike (more than 200 hikers per day), the NPS has established special regulations. The trail is open only from 5 a.m. to 9 p.m., and pets, bicycles, soap, food or beverages, and public nudity are prohibited. You can only swim in the Gardner River, not in the hot spring where it emerges from under a travertine ledge.

Another unusual tidbit of information is that this trail starts exactly at the 45th Parallel, precisely halfway between the North Pole and the Equator.

Options: You can also hike down to the Boiling River from the Mammoth Campground, but this is a much tougher hike involving a 300-foot hill to get back to the campground.

Boiling River, Bunsen Peak, Beaver Ponds

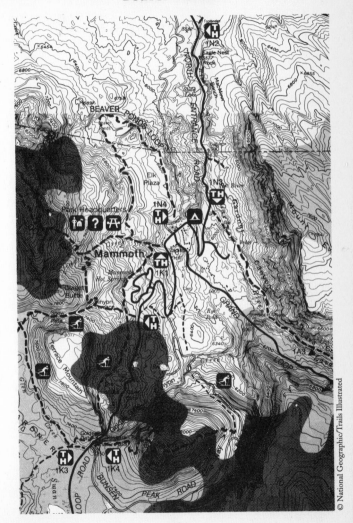

7

BUNSEN PEAK ✗

Type of hike: Out-and-back.
Total distance: 4.2 miles or 6.7 kilometers (round-trip).
Elevation gain: 1,300 feet.
Maps: Trails Illustrated; Mammoth Hot Springs and Mammoth USGS Quads.
Starting point: Bunsen Peak Creek Trailhead (1K4).
Finding the trailhead: Drive 4.7 miles south of Mammoth on the Mammoth-Norris section of the Grand Loop Road to just past the Golden Gate Bridge and park on the left (east) in the Glen Creek Trailhead parking lot.

The hike: This trail offers the easiest way to get a spectacular mountaintop view of the northwestern corner of the park. However some people wouldn't call this an easy hike. You go up 1,300 feet in 2.1 miles. Fortunately the trail is superbly switchbacked to minimize the impact of the elevation gain. In addition, the scenery along the way tends to absorb you so you don't focus on the effort it takes to reach the summit. If you want to be able to say you climbed a mountain in Yellowstone Park, this hike (or Mount Washburn) would be your least strenuous way to meet that goal.

Be sure to bring water, though. You won't find any on the mountain unless you hike in June or early July when you can find snowbanks.

From the top, you can see the large meadow below to the west known as Gardners Hole and of course, a river runs through it (the Gardner River). You can also see the town of Gardiner over the top of Terrace Mountain along with Mammoth Terrace in the foreground—and awesome 10,992-foot Electric Peak to the west, 10,336-foot Mount Holmes to the south, the mighty Absarokas to the north, and just about everything else. The telecommunications equipment on the summit is somewhat distracting, but the view is undeniably overwhelming.

You might want to hike this early in the morning before the afternoon heat makes the climb harder. If you go early, bring along some binoculars so you can watch wildlife from the summit.

8
BEAVER PONDS

see map on page 19

Type of hike: Loop.
Total distance: 5.1 miles or 8.2 kilometers.
Elevation gain: 226 feet.
Maps: Trails Illustrated; Mammoth Hot Springs and Mammoth USGS Quads.
Starting point: Sepulcher Mountain Trailhead (1K1) in Mammoth.
Finding the trailhead: Drive south from Gardiner to Mammoth Hot Springs. The trailhead is on the right (west) just below the main hot springs by Liberty Cap.

Key points:
0.2 (0.3) Junction with Howard Eaton Trail.
0.7 (1.6) Junction with Sepulcher Mountain Trail.
3.0 (4.8) Beaver Ponds.
5.0 (8.0) Intersection with old road.
5.1 (8.1) Mammoth.

The hike: If you stay at Mammoth and have some extra time to get away from the traffic-choked roads, this gentle 5-mile loop trail is a good option. There is an excellent chance of seeing elk (if you haven't already seen enough right in Mammoth), moose, and black bear.

The trail begins just to the right (north) of Clematis Creek before Liberty Cap. Ordinarily you could park and start at

22

the same trailhead as the boardwalk trail around the hot springs, but the footbridge didn't survive the high water of the spring of 1996. When we did this hike, it was necessary to start from the bus parking area on the east side of the creek.

The trail starts out gradually uphill with brilliant colors of Mammoth Hot Springs on the left (south). Then the trail crosses Clematis Creek on a bridge that did survive the high water.

At 0.2 mile you reach the junction with the Golden Gate/Howard Eaton Trail, which takes you behind the hot springs and to Terrace Mountain. Turn right (west) and continue toward Beaver Ponds. The trail crosses another bridge and climbs more steeply, passing one unmarked junction with a game trail. Stay right and keep switchbacking uphill.

At 0.7 mile turn right (north) at the junction with the Sepulcher Ridge Trail. The junction has a unique marker. An old carved stump signals, "Mountain Trail/Ranger Nature Trail." That old nature trail is now called the Beaver Ponds Trail.

After this junction the trail levels out and crosses meadows of dandelions and aspen with bark chewed off by winter-starved elk. In the spring you might see some larkspur and shooting stars along the way. The section of trail offers sweeping views of Gardner River Valley and across to the Absaroka Range to the north.

After a short descent, the trail passes the first of several ponds. The Beaver Ponds consist of several marshy lakes graced by cattails and a few lily pads.

The return trip is relatively flat across a sagebrush

plateau with good scenery all around, especially Mount Everts (which would be better described as a ridge) across Gardner Canyon. When you see the town of Mammoth, the trail intersects an old road. Again, stay right. This last 0.1-mile descent to Mammoth terminates behind the main lodge where you can make your way back to the trailhead.

Northeast Region

9
TROUT LAKE

Type of hike: Out-and-back.
Type of hike: 1.2 miles or 1.9 kilometers (round-trip).
Elevation gain: 100 feet.
Maps: Trails Illustrated; Tower/Canyon and Mount Hornaday USGS Quads.
Starting point: Trout Lake Trailhead.
Finding the trailhead: Drive 18.6 miles east of Tower Junction or 10.4 miles west of the Northeast Entrance and park in the turnout on the north side of the road, 1.8 miles west of Pebble Creek Campground.

The hike: This trail is popular with anglers in the Lamar Valley, but it also provides a pleasant day hike for non-anglers. The rainbow-cutthroat hybrids in the lake are big and hard to catch but incredibly rewarding for the successful angler.

From the trailhead, the trail heads steeply uphill. The path climbs under Douglas-fir cover to the inlet of the lake, which rests in a big meadow filled with wildflowers. The trail around the lake prvides more hiking.

The 12-acre lake is catch-and-release fishing (don't forget to get a park fishing permit). But the inlet is closed to fishing to protect spawning trout, which provide quite the show for onlookers. But be careful not to disturb the spawners at this crucial time.

Trout Lake

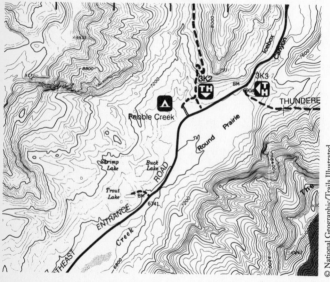

© National Geographic/Trails Illustrated

10
HELLROARING CREEK

Type of hike: Out-and-back.
Total distance: 4 miles or 6.4 kilometers (round-trip).
Elevation gain: 600 feet.
Maps: Trails Illustrated; Tower/Canyon and Tower Junction USGS Quads.
Starting point: Hellroaring Trailhead (2K8).
Finding the trailhead: Drive 14.5 miles east of Mammoth or 3.5 miles west of Tower on the Mammoth-Tower section of the Grand Loop Road and pull into a service road on the north side of the road. The trailhead is about a half mile farther at the end of the road.

Key points:
0.8 (1.3)   Junction with trail to Tower.
1.0 (1.6)   Suspension Bridge.
1.6 (2.6)   Junction with trail to Coyote Creek and Buffalo
            Plateau.
2.0 (3.2)   Hellroaring Creek.

The hike: This is the first part of the longer hikes through the Black Canyon of the Yellowstone and around the Hellroaring Creek and Coyote Creek Loop. In addition to making a nice day hike, this section of trail is a great choice for the beginning backpacker who has the choice of six excellent campsites on Hellroaring Creek..

The trail switchbacks through open timber and sagebrush meadows for the first mile to the suspension bridge over the Yellowstone River. This isn't the suspension bridge you saw

Hellroaring Creek

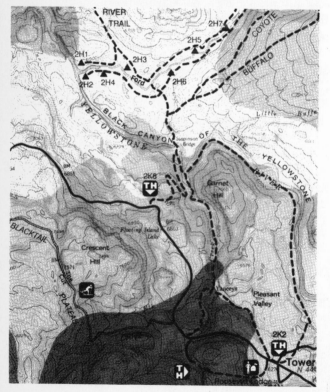

© National Geographic/Trails Illustrated

in the Indiana Jones movies. It's steel and very sturdy. From the bridge, the trail goes into the open landscape in the Yellowstone and Hellroaring valleys.

The trail is in superb condition all the way. You pass by two trail junctions, the first to Tower and the second up Coyote Creek. Go left (west) at both junctions.

11
YELLOWSTONE RIVER PICNIC AREA TRAIL

see map on page 34

Type of hike: Out-and-back.
Total distance: 4 miles or 6.4 kilometers (round-trip).
Elevation gain: 200 feet.
Maps: Trails Illustrated; Tower/Canyon and Tower Junction USGS Quads.
Starting point: Yellowstone River Picnic Area Trailhead (2K7).
Finding the trailhead: Drive 1.5 miles east of Tower Junction and pull into the picnic area on the south side of the road.

The hike: This is a delightful day hike when you need some exercise after a picnic. You can go as far as 2 miles before the trail joins the Specimen Ridge Trail, or you can walk along the ridge overlooking the Yellowstone for whatever distance suits you before returning to the picnic area.

Several social trails leave the picnic area, and they join up with the official trail about a half mile later. The official trail starts by the trail sign on the east side of the picnic area and appears to head east, but it quickly turns south and gradually climbs up to the ridge above the river.

After a short climb the trail levels out and goes along the rim of the Yellowstone—great scenery, but if you have children, watch them carefully. It would be a very serious fall down into the river bottom.

12
LOST LAKE

see map on page 34

Type of hike: Out-and-back, loop or shuttle.
Total distance: 2.5 miles or 4 kilometers (loop).
Elevation gain: 200 feet.
Maps: Trails Illustrated; Tower/Canyon and Tower Junction USGS Quads.
Starting point: Roosevelt Lodge.
Finding the trailhead: From Tower Junction drive south into the Roosevelt Lodge and park near the lodge. The trail starts at the south edge of the lodge.

The hike: Lost Lake is a charming little (only 6 acres) mountain lake lost in the forest behind Roosevelt Lodge.

From the lodge the trail gradually climbs through unburned forest on gentle switchbacks about 200 feet up to the top of the ridge where you reach a junction. The left trail goes east to Lost Creek Falls and Tower Campground. Go right (west) for about another half mile to Lost Lake, which is preceded by a big meadow. The lake is shallow with yellow pond lilies along the shoreline. Sorry, no fish.

From the lake keep going east until you come out in the parking lot for the Petrified Tree. You can drive here, but by walking down from the lake you can avoid retracing your steps and make a small loop out of this hike. When we hiked this trail, there was no sign marking the cutoff trail that follows the Mammoth-Tower Road back to Roosevelt

Lodge, but this well-defined, heavily used trail starts on the other side of the parking lot from where you come in from Lost Lake. It's marked with an orange marker.

Options: If you want to make this a shorter hike, walk out and back to the lake. If you want a shuttle (and a good view of Lost Creek Falls) take a left at the top of the ridge and hike another 3 miles to Tower Fall Campground. The trail comes out on the paved road up to the campground. You can walk down the road about a quarter mile to the general store. This is a nice, flat trail through open forest and large meadows until it drops steeply down to the campground.

13
TOWER FALL

Type of hike: Out-and-back.
Total distance: 1 mile or 1.6 kilometers (round-trip).
Elevation gain: 200 feet.
Maps: Trails Illustrated; Tower/Canyon and Tower Junction USGS Quads.
Starting point: Tower Fall store.
Finding the trailhead: Drive 2.5 miles south of Tower Junction or 15.5 miles north of Canyon Junction on the Tower-Canyon section of the Grand Loop Road and park in the large parking lot for the Tower Fall store.

The hike: The trip to Tower Fall is one of the shortest but most-rewarding hikes in the park. From the overlook (about 100 yards from the store), you get a great perspective of the 132-foot waterfall. Then by walking down a double-wide, carefully switchbacked trail for another half mile, you get the rest of the story.

The trail takes you right down to where Tower Creek disappears into the Yellowstone. Then with a short walk to your left, walk right to the foot of the falls, a truly awesome sight.

Take along a sweater. Even on a warm August afternoon, the mist thrown up by the falls can cast a cool atmosphere over the shaded canyon gouged out by the crashing water. The 1870 Washburn party named the waterfall for the large tower-like rocks at the brink of the falls, one of which crashed to the depths of the canyon in 1986. No, luckily, there weren't any park visitors under the falls at the time!

Yellowstone Picnic Area Trail, Lost Lake, Tower Fall

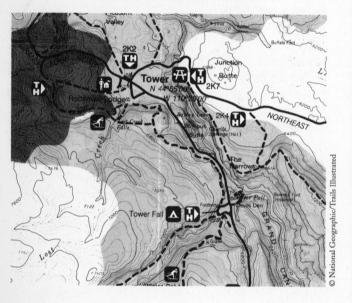

© National Geographic/Trails Illustrated

14
MOUNT WASHBURN

Type of hike: Out-and-back.
Total distance: 5.2 miles or 8.3 kilometers.
Elevation gain: 1,491 feet.
Maps: Trails Illustrated; Tower/Canyon and Mount Washburn USGS Quads.
Starting point: Chittenden Road Trailhead (2K6).
Finding the trailhead: Drive 5.5 miles north of Canyon or 13.5 miles south of Tower on the Tower-Canyon section of the Grand Loop Road and turn onto the well-marked Chittenden Road. Follow the gravel road for about a mile to a locked gate and a large parking lot off to the left.

The hike: The Chittenden Road continues up to the top of the mountain, but it's for official use only. You have to walk or ride a mountain bike to the summit.

It's nearly 1,500 feet to the top of what is left of an ancient volcano that exploded 600,000 years ago and created the Yellowstone Caldera. However, the slope of the gravel road (made for vehicles, of course) makes for easy walking. Very few vehicles use the road, so it seems like a big, wide trail.

You hike in the open slopes of Mount Washburn the entire way. If you don't see bighorn sheep on the way up, you almost assuredly will see them on the summit where a small herd resides most of the summer. (Please don't feed

Mount Washburn

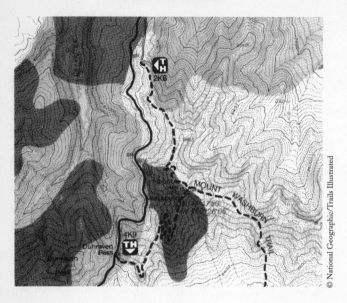

© National Geographic/Trails Illustrated

them!) Also expect to be hiking through a virtual wildflower bouquet the entire way. Mount Washburn yearly hosts an incredible abundance and diversity of alpine wildflowers. After hiking all of Yellowstone, I did not find another place that matched the wildflower showcase found on Mount Washburn.

At the summit you might be surprised to find a major structure conservatively referred to as a lookout. It has an interpretive center, 20-power telescopes for wildlife viewing, drinking fountain, bathrooms, and even a pay phone.

Watch the weather. You don't want to get caught on this mountain in a thunderstorm.

Options: You can also come up to the summit of Mount Washburn from Dunraven Pass, which is about the same distance and intensity as the Chittenden Road route but slightly harder on the nerves as it goes along a knife-edge ridge just before the summit.

Side trips: If you have some extra time on top, you can walk along the ridge toward Dunraven Pass for about a half mile without losing much elevation. You can also hike the first part of the spur trail to Canyon, which heads off to the east through a major wildflower garden. If you want to identify every flower along the way, you'll need several hours.

15
CASCADE LAKE

Type of hike: Out-and-back.
Total distance: 5 miles or 8 kilometers.
Elevation gain: Minimal
Maps: Trails Illustrated; Tower/Canyon, Mammoth Hot Springs, Crystal Falls, Cook Peak, Canyon Village, and Mount Washburn USGS Quads.
Starting point: Cascade Lake Trail Picnic Area (4K5).
Finding the trailhead: Drive 1.3 miles north of Canyon Junction and park in the parking area on the west side of the road.

Key points:
2.0 (3.2)   Junction with Cascade Creek Trail.
2.3 (3.7)   Spur Trail to backcountry campsite 4E4.
2.4 (3.8)   Junction with trail to Observation Peak and backcountry campsite 4E3.
2.5 (4.0)   Cascade Lake.

The hike: This is a great choice for the beginning backpacker looking for one of his or her first nights in the wilderness. This also makes a nice day hike after an enjoyable picnic at the trailhead.

It's a short 2.5 miles to the large, deep lake, and the trail is in excellent condition the entire way and even double-wide near the picnic area. It's a nice flat hike through scattered forest and meadows until you get close to the lake and enter a huge meadow. In June and July the meadows along the way are ablaze with wildflowers—and full of bison, too, so be careful.

The 36-acre lake has a heathly population of cutthroat and grayling, so expect to see a few anglers throwing artifical flies into the lake.

Options: You can also get to Cascade Lake from the Cascade Creek Trailhead (4K4). It's about the same distance and

Cascade Lake

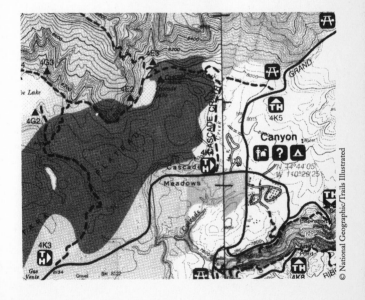

© National Geographic/Trails Illustrated

gradient, but this route receives heavy use from commercial horse parties. If you're looking for an easy overnighter, Cascade Lake is a good choice.

Side trips: If you have time you can hike from the lake 3 miles up to the summit of Observation Peak. You can also take the 2.5-mile hike over to Grebe Lake.

16
CANYON RIM SOUTH

see map on page 46

Type of hike: Out-and-back or shuttle.
Total distance: 3.2 miles or 5.2 kilometers (one way).
Elevation gain: 150 feet.
Maps: The Yellowstone Association's map/brochure for Canyon, Trails Illustrated; Tower/Canyon and Canyon Village USGS Quads.
Starting point: Wapiti Lake Trailhead (4K7).
Finding the trailhead: Drive south 2.3 miles from the Canyon Junction, turn left (east), crossing the Chittenden Bridge, and park in the large parking area on your right immediately after crossing the bridge.

The hike: There are two ways to see the sights of the South Rim of the Grand Canyon of the Yellowstone. You can drive from parking lot to parking lot, get in and out of your car several times, and call it a day. Or you can take a wonderful hike along the canyon rim to see it all and get some exercise, too.

The trail from Chittenden Bridge to Point Sublime is 3.5 miles. You can take all of it or whatever section that suits you.

The scenery is world-renown the entire way with many views of the mighty Yellowstone River and its Grand Canyon, Lower Falls and Upper Falls, all the way to Point Sublime, and a view of Silver Cord Cascades plunging down into the canyon from Ribbon Lake.

The trail gets very heavy use, and parts of it are paved to accommodate this popularity. Even the unpaved sections are in superb condition. Unless you go down the Uncle Tom's Trail, there aren't any steep sections, although you face a few short upgrades to get through small valleys and a gradual upgrade to get from the river-level trailhead to Artists Point Overlook, about 150 feet above the river.

From the trailhead the trail drops down to river-level right above Upper Falls where you get a good view of the foot-bridge on the other side of the river. Just before Uncle Tom's Trail parking area, you get the ideal view of Upper Falls from the Upper Falls Overlook. At Artists Point you get the picturesque view of Lower Falls and the Grand Canyon. If you stop at Artist Point, you'll miss one of the great views in the park, Point Sublime. The grand expansiveness of the canyon is spread before you at Point Sublime.

If you can't arrange to leave a vehicle, retrace your steps to the Wapiti Lake Trailhead.

Options: You can hike sections of this trail out and back or you can leave a vehicle at Artists Point to keep from retracing your steps over part of the trip. You can also combine the South Rim and North Rim hikes by leaving a vehicle at Inspiration Point and starting at Artists Point or vice versa.

Side trips: Uncle Tom's Trail is a must-see side trip. This may be the most unusual hike in the park. It's not really a trail. Instead it's a series of stairs made of steel grates, concrete, and asphalt, 328 steps from top to bottom. The "grand staircase" takes you down 500 feet in elevation to an incredible viewpoint near the base of the Lower Falls. The trail gets its name from "Uncle" Tom Richardson who took park visitors into the canyon from 1898 to 1903 on this trail, which was originally 528 steps and rope ladders.

Although short (1 mile round-trip), the trail can be quite strenuous coming up and is not recommended for anybody with heart or lung problems. However, the NPS has made it as easy as possible with handrails much of the way and benches to rest on while climbing out of the canyon.

17
CANYON RIM NORTH

Type of hike: Out-and-back or shuttle.
Total distance: 3 miles or 4.8 kilometers (one way).
Elevation gain: 150 feet.
Maps: The Yellowstone Association's map/brochure for Canyon, Trails Illustrated; Tower/Canyon and Canyon Village USGS Quads.
Starting point: Wapiti Lake Trailhead (4K7).
Finding the trailhead: Drive south 2.3 miles from the Canyon Junction, turn left (east), crossing the Chittenden Bridge, and park in the large parking area on your right immediately after crossing the bridge.

The hike: Like the South Rim, the North Rim is loaded with world-famous scenery and short side trips. It's a nice half-day hike if you take in all the sights.

From the bridge, hike to the short (about a quarter mile) side trip to the Brink of the Upper Falls, an awe-inspiring (if not scary) view of the river plunging over the 109-foot Upper Falls.

Next along the way is Crystal Falls on Cascade Creek, a nice contrast to the Upper and Lower Falls. The trails goes over the top of the delicate waterfall. Then you reach perhaps the most memorable spot on the trip—the side trip down to the Brink of the Lower Falls where you can really feel the power of the mighty Yellowstone as in tumbles over the massive 308-foot waterfall, the tallest in the park..

About a half mile down the trail is the side trip to Lookout Point and Red Rock Point. Both give additional views of Lower Falls. Lookout Point is a 50-foot walk, but Red Rock Point requires a steep quarter-mile drop.

Next at Grandview Point you get one more version of the Lower Falls and Grand Canyon vista. The trail is mostly paved up to this point, but from here to Inspiration Point you hike on a normal unpaved trail. Inspiration Point offers one more perspective of Lower Falls, but it includes the broad sweep of the Grand Canyon in the foreground. The Grand Canyon varies from 1,500 feet to 4,000 feet across and from 750 to 1,200 feet deep. Hot springs in the area weakened the rock and caused extreme erosion below Lower Falls to create the Grand Canyon.

Options: You can hike sections of this trail out and back or you can leave a vehicle at Inspiration Point to keep from retracing your steps. You can also combine the North Rim and South Rim hikes by leaving a vehicle at Inspiration Point and starting at Artists Point or vice versa.

Side trips: Short side trips to Brink of the Upper Falls, Brink of the Lower Falls, Lookout Point, and Red Rock Point add to this hike. Uncle Tom's Trail on the South Rim is the toughest climb down into the canyon. Red Rock Point is next toughest, followed by Brink of the Lower Falls.

If you only take one of these side trips, Brink of the Lower Falls would probably be your most rewarding choice. At the end of the 0.75-mile trip (one way) to a concrete platform above the falls, you can't avoid the sensation of being over-powered by nature. The earth (and the platform) seems to quiver as the mighty river plunges over the 308-foot water-fall, the highest waterfall in the park..

The trail is steep (600 feet elevation loss) and includes several sections of stairs. It's not recommended for people with lung or heart problems—but highly recommended for anybody with an average fitness level. An interpretive dis-play on the platform tells the story of how Lower Falls came to be.

Canyon Rim North, Canyon Rim South, Ribbon Lake

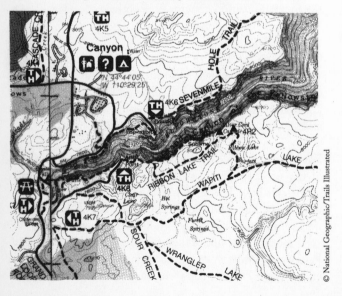

© National Geographic/Trails Illustrated

18
RIBBON LAKE

see map on page 46

Type of hike: Out-and-back.
Total distance: 4 miles or 6.4 kilometers (round-trip).
Elevation gain: Minimal.
Maps: Trails Illustrated; Tower/Canyon and Canyon Village USGS Quad.
Starting point: Artist Point Trailhead (4K8).
Finding the trailhead: Drive south 2.3 miles past Canyon Junction and turn left, crossing the Chittenden Bridge, and go 1 mile until the road terminates at the heavily used Artist Point Viewpoint. The trail starts on the right as you walk down to the viewpoint.

Key Points:
0.5 (0.8)   Sublime Point junction.
1.0 (1.6)   Junction with trail to Clear Lake.
2.0 (3.2)   Ribbon Lake Camps 4R1 and 4R2.

The hike: The trail from Artist Point is the perfect hike for someone just getting in to overnight camping and hiking. You aren't that far from the trailhead, and the hike in is easy walking. In addition, Ribbon Lake has a small population of rainbow trout (catch-and-release only with a park fishing permit). You can also have a campfire, and this trip has several possible side trips, one of which can give you a view that rivals that from Artist Point. The trail is in excellent shape the entire way.

At Artist Point, the trail leaves the paved area before the viewpoint and takes off to the right (northeast) toward Sublime Point. The trail climbs along the edge of the canyon with an incredible, already-sublime view. At 0.5 mile turn right (south) and leave the trail to Sublime Point and head for Ribbon Lake—unless you want to take a short side trip to the Sublime Point before going to Ribbon Lake.

In less than a half mile is the junction with the trail to Clear Lake where you turn left (northeast). Some maps may not show this junction.

After the junction the trail is flat and stays in the trees until you reach Ribbon Lake, which is actually two lakes connected by a foot-deep, narrow channel. The smaller lake is surrounded by sedge meadows and may be completely covered with yellow pond lilies.

At Ribbon Lake a spur trail veers left to backcountry campsites 4R1 and 4R2 and to the Silver Cord Cascade overlook. Even if you aren't camping take the short side trip on this trail for a view of the cascade and the Grand Canyon of the Yellowstone. The cascade is a waterfall off the edge of the canyon. It's eerie to suddenly emerge from the trees and look down at the river hundreds of feet below. The forest offers no clue that you're so close to the edge.

Side trips: Two short, must-see side trips are Sublime Point and the Silver Cord Cascade overlook.

Southwest Region

19
SENTINEL MEADOWS

Type of hike: Out-and-back.
Total distance: 3.8 miles or 6.1 kilometers (round-trip).
Elevation gain: Minimal.
Maps: Trails Illustrated; Old Faithful and Lower Geyser Basin USGS Quads.
Starting point: Sentinel Meadows Trailhead (OK6).
Finding the trailhead: Drive 6.1 miles south of Madison Junction or 9.9 miles north of Old Faithful on the Madison-Old Faithful section of the Grand Loop Road. Turn west onto Fountain Flat Drive and park in a large parking area about a half mile from the main road. At this point, Fountain Flat Drive is barricaded, so you walk on the road for about another quarter mile to the official trailhead on your right (west) just after crossing the Firehole River Bridge.

Key points:
0.2 (0.3)   Ojo Caliente Spring.
0.3 (0.5)   Firehole River Bridge and Sentinel Meadows
            Trailhead (OK6)

1.0 (1.6)   OG1.
1.5 (2.4)   Junction with trail from Imperial Meadows
            Trailhead (OK8)
1.9 (3.0)   Sentinel Meadows and Queens Laundry.

The hike: The first 0.3 mile of this hike is on the closed section of Fountain Flat Drive. Just before crossing the Firehole River, you go by Ojo Caliente Spring (Spanish for "hot spring"), which is only one of the interesting thermal areas along this trail.

Sentinel Meadows, Fairy Falls

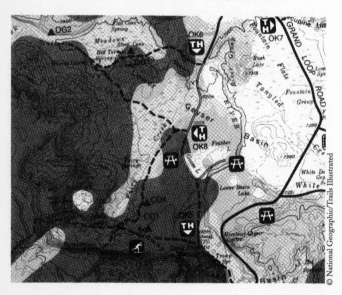

© National Geographic/Trails Illustrated

The trail stays in great shape (flat and easy to follow) all the way to the junction with the trail coming in from Imperial Meadows. Watch for bison on the trail and give them a wide berth.

At the junction, the trail starts to rapidly deteriorate. In short order, it disappears into the massive Sentinel Meadows just past a major thermal area called Queens Laundry, where early explorers bathed and, yes, did their laundry. Please don't try either today. Regulations prevent this, and early use of the area destroyed some incredibly colorful terraces. You might also see the remains of an old bathhouse built in 1881 and rumored to be the first building meant to serve the public ever built in any national park.

At this point, retrace your steps to the trailhead. After Queens Laundry the trail melts into a huge marsh. Even in August, you can't cross anywhere without walking through water and muck.

Options: This hike also makes an easy overnighter for beginning backpackers.

20
FAIRY FALLS

see map on page 50

Type of hike: Out-and-back.
Total distance: 3.6 miles or 5.8 kilometers (round-trip).
Elevation gain: Minimal.
Starting point: Fairy Falls Trailhead (OK5).
Finding the trailhead: Drive 5.5 miles south of Madison Junction or 10.5 miles north of Old Faithful on the Madison-Old Faithful section of the Grand Loop Road and turn into the parking area on the west side of the road just south of the Grand Prismatic Spring. The trail starts across a jeep road bridge on Fountain Flats Drive, which is closed to cars but open to mountain bikes.

Key points:
0.8 (1.2)   Junction with Fairy Falls Trail.
1.4 (2.2)   Spur trail to OD1.
1.6 (2.5)   Fairy Falls.

The hike: This a short, easy hike to a falls more mystic than Mystic Falls.

From the trailhead walk on Fountain Flats Drive as it crosses the Firehole River on a bridge and skirts the west side of the Midway Geyser Basin, with Grand Prismatic Spring off to the right (east). In less than a mile the Fairy Falls Trail turns left (west) off the road. The trail is well-traveled and easy to follow as it goes through burnt lodgepole.

Fairy Falls is a delicate, 197-foot waterfall named for its graceful beauty. There's a bridge below the falls, and a short spur trail allows you to get an even closer look at the falls and the deep pool it has carved out.

After enjoying a nice break at the falls, retrace your steps to the trailhead.

21
MYSTIC FALLS

see map on page 57

Type of hike: Loop.
Total distance: 3 miles or 4.8 kilometers (round-trip).
Elevation gain: 700 feet.
Maps: Yellowstone Association's Old Faithful map/brochure; Trails Illustrated; Old Faithful and Old Faithful USGS Quads.
Starting point: Biscuit Basin Trailhead (OK4).
Finding the trailhead: Drive 2 miles north of Old Faithful or 14 miles south of Madison Junction and park in the Biscuit Basin Boardwalk parking area on the west side of the road.

Key points:

0.6 (1.0)	Junction with Summit Lake Trail.
0.8 (1.2)	Junction with Mystic Falls Trail.
1.1 (1.8)	Mystic Falls.
1.7 (2.7)	Junction with Fairy Creek Trail.
2.0 (3.2)	Mystic Falls Overlook
2.2 (3.5)	Junction with Little Firehole Meadows Trail.
3.0 (4.8)	Biscuit Basin Trailhead.

The trail: Mystic Falls is a popular day hike destination from Old Faithful and hence receives heavy use. It's a short, easy, and beautiful hike with incredible views of a cascading, 100-foot waterfall, Biscuit Basin, and the Old Faithful area.

From the parking area follow the the Biscuit Basin Boardwalk around to the right until you reach the Little Firehole Meadows Trail. Go right (west) here and stay right (west) again when you pass the junction with the trail to Summit Lake about a quarter mile down the trail. Next is the junction with the Mystic Falls loop trail, which joins from the right. Stay left for the quickest route to the falls. You can return on the overlook route.

At 1.1 mile is Mystic Falls where the Little Firehole River suddenly leaves the Madison Plateau and drops into Biscuit Basin. Past Mystic Falls the trail climbs abruptly to the junction with the trail from Fairy Creek. Turn right (east) here and hike another quarter mile or so to an overlook (with safety fence) and sweeping view to the east of Old Faithful and the Firehole River.

After soaking in the view for awhile continue east of the overlook, dropping steeply until you rejoin the Mystic Falls Trail. Then retrace your steps to the trailhead.

22
UPPER GEYSER BASIN

Type of hike: Loop.
Total distance: Varies from 1.5 (2.4 kilometers) to 5 miles (8 kilometers), depending on which loop you hike.
Elevation gain: Minimal unless you go to Geyser Hill, an easy 250-foot climb.
Maps: Yellowstone Association's Old Faithful map/brochure; Trails Illustrated; Old Faithful and Old Faithful USGS Quads.
Starting point: Old Faithful Visitor Center.
Finding the trailhead: Drive 16 miles south of Madison Junction or 17 miles west of West Thumb and take the Old Faithful exit. Follow the signs to the visitor center.

The hike: When you hear people talking about day hiking in Yellowstone, they usually talk about geysers and other thermal areas, and they are probably talking about this hike. This trail goes by an almost unimaginable number of fascinating thermal features. But don't expect to be alone in the wilderness. This may also be the most heavily used trail in the park.

Be sure to spend a quarter at the visitor center for a well-done brochure and map of the area published by The Yellowstone Association. This brochure is much better than any other map of the area.

Mystic Falls, Upper Geyser Basin

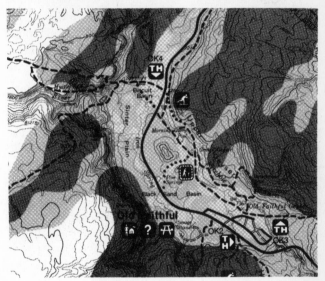

Unlike most other hikes, this loop offers several options in length to suit your physical ability and mood of the day. Also much of the trail is on boardwalks and paved walkways accessible to wheelchairs. The trail and walkway on the south side of the Firehole River is open to bicycles.

The longest route includes the Geyser Hill Loop and goes from the visitor center to the Biscuit Basin Trailhead, along the Grand Loop Road for less than a quarter mile and then back on the other side of the Firehole River. This long route includes about 2 miles of regular trails in addition to the boardwalks and walkways.

You can shorten the loop by crossing over the Firehole River on bridges near the Morning Glory Pool (2.8-mile trip) or Grand Geyser or Castle Geyser (1.4-mile loop). Adding the Geyser Hill loop lengthens the trip by 1.3 miles.

All Upper Geyser Basin hikes start out with a bang—the eruption of Old Faithful, which erupts an average of every 79 minutes, more frequently than any other big geyser. You can view this famous phenomenon from benches in front of the visitor center, or if you have time, you can get a more distant view from Geyser Hill—or if you time your hike correctly, both.

It pays to study the map carefully before taking off. The entire trip is on superb trails, walkways, or boardwalks. Even the trip up to the Geyser Hill Viewpoint is in excellent shape with well-planned switchbacks, making the small climb seem easy.

Regardless of how much of the area you choose to hike, set aside much more time than you would normally allow for a hike of this length. Speed is not an issue on this hike. Instead, the NPS has provided an incredible educational experience with frequent interpretive signs, brochures, and guided tours. Interpretive rangers normally hike the area and can answer your questions. If you're interested in a ranger-led tour, inquire at the visitor center for the schedule.

23
LONE STAR GEYSER

Type of hike: Out-and-back with loop option.
Total distance: 4.6 miles or 7.4 kilometers (round-trip).
Elevation gain: Minimal.
Maps: Trails Illustrated; Old Faithful and Old Faithful USGS Quads.
Starting point: Lone Star Trailhead (OK1).
Finding the trailhead: Drive east of the Old Faithful interchange 3.5 miles on the Old Faithful-West Thumb section of the Grand Loop Road and park at the Lone Star Trailhead on the south side of the road.

The hike: This is a fairly level hike to a well-known and heavily visited geyser. Lone Star Geyser is so popular that the NPS has paved the trail and opened it to mountain bikers. Even though you might see a few bikers and more than a few hikers on this trail, it's still a pleasant hike along the Upper Firehole River. About a half mile before the geyser stay right (south) at the junction with the Spring Creek Trail, continuing on the paved path. The pavement ends about 100 feet before the geyser and is blocked by downed trees to discourage bicycle traffic beyond this point.

Lone Star Geyser was named for its isolated location (5 miles south of Old Faithful with no other geysers in the neighborhood). The name has nothing to do with Texas, the Lone Star State. It erupts 30 to 50 feet every 2 to 3 hours or so for about 10 to 15 minutes. Gurgling sounds come from the geyser's large cone between eruptions.

Options: If you don't want to hike on a paved trail with mountain bikers, you can hike to Lone Star Geyser out and back from Fern Cascades Trailhead (OK2), which is about 1.7 miles north of the Lone Star Trailhead. This lengthens the round-trip to 6.4 miles.

You can also start this hike at Fern Cascades Trailhead and come out at Lone Start Trailhead or vice versa. This requires two vehicles or a 1.7-mile walk on the highway to get back to your vehicle. Total distance of the loop is 7.2 miles.

Lone Star Geyser

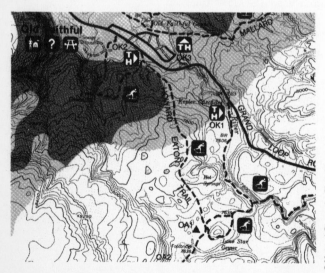

© National Geographic/Trails Illustrated

24
BEULA LAKE

Type of hike: Out-and-back.
Total distance: 6 miles or 9.6 kilometers (round-trip).
Elevation gain: Minimal.
Maps: Trails Illustrated; Old Faithful and Grassy Lake Reservoir USGS Quads.
Starting point: East end of Grassy Reservoir.
Finding the trailhead: Drive 10 miles west of Flagg Ranch (2 miles south of the park on U.S. 287) on a mostly unpaved road to Grassy Reservoir. The trailhead is not marked, but it's a steep pullout on the north side of the road just before you reach the reservoir.

The hike: From the trailhead the trail gradually climbs over a small ridge and drops to Beula Lake. The trail is in superb condition the entire way. It goes though partly burned forest, but the lakeshore itself has not been burned.

About a half mile from the trailhead, the trail crosses the South Boundary Trail. When we hiked this trail, there was no sign at this junction. Be careful not to turn either way on the South Boundary Trail. Instead go straight (north) to Beula Lake.

Beula Lake (named after a mystical land of sunshine and delight) is a fairly large (107 acres) lake with two designated campsites. It hosts a healthy cutthroat population and is popular with anglers.

Options: This hike also makes a nice overnighter for beginning backpackers or anglers.

Beula Lake

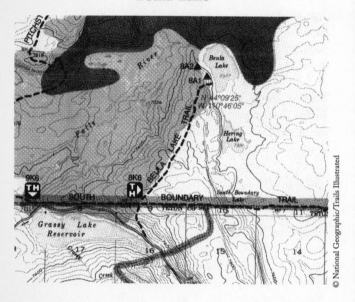

Southeast region

25
STORM POINT

Type of hike: Loop.
Total distance: 1.5 miles or 2.4 kilometers (round-trip).
Elevation gain: Minimal.
Maps: Trails Illustrated; Yellowstone Lake and Lake Butte USGS Quads.
Starting point: Storm Point Trailhead by Indian Pond.
Finding the trailhead: Drive 3.1 miles east of Fishing Bridge Junction and park in the small parking area on the south side of the road about a half mile after crossing Pelican Creek.

The hike: If you like a ranger-led interpretive hike where you can really learn about the human and natural history of the Yellowstone Lake area, check at the Fishing Bridge Visitor Center or Lake Ranger Station for a schedule of trips on the Storm Point Trail. You can also take the hike anytime you feel the urge without an official guide—and many people do. This is a delightful evening stroll after driving around or working all day. The nearly level trail is in great shape.

The trail starts out by going by the west edge of Indian Pond, a popular bird-watching site in the Lake area. The

Storm Point

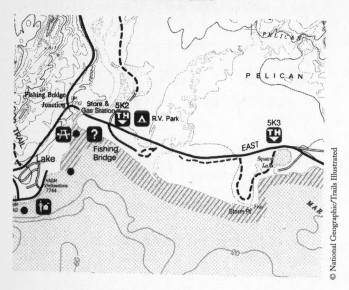

pond gets its name because it served as a historic camping area for Indian tribes.

After going by the pond, the trail goes through a short section of timber before taking a swing to the right and to Storm Point, a small rocky peninsula that juts out into the lake, named because it gets seriously whipped by storms moving northeasterly through the park.

After Storm Point the trail follows the lakeshore, offering constant scenic views of the lake for about a half mile before turning right through timber and clouds of mosquitoes (in June and July) back to the highway. The trail breaks out into the same large meadow you started in just before reaching the road. Walk about a quarter mile along the road back to your vehicle.

26
NATURAL BRIDGE

see map on page 69

Type of hike: Out-and-back.
Total distance: 2.5 miles or 4 kilometers (round-trip).
Elevation gain: Minimal.
Maps: Trails Illustrated Yellowstone Lake and Lake USGS Quad.
Starting point: Bridge Bay Marina parking lot.
Finding the trailhead: Drive 2 miles south of Lake on the Lake-West Thumb section of the Grand Loop Road and turn west into the Bridge Bay Marina. Go another 0.4 miles and turn left into the parking lot.

The hike: You used to be able to drive to Natural Bridge, but the NPS has converted the trip into a short day hike. This hike is the mirror image of most trails. It starts out as a super trail and gets better instead of worse. You begin on a single track, go to a double-wide trail, and finish on a paved road.

From the marina parking lot look for a trail sign and a paved trail heading west toward the campground. Just as you reach the campground, the trail takes a sharp left (south), so be careful not to miss this turn.

From here walk through unburned forest on an abandoned road along the west side of Bridge Bay for about a half mile to a paved road (now closed to motor vehicles but still open to bicycles). Turn right (west) and follow the road for another half mile or so until it ends with a little loop, which goes by Natural Bridge.

An interpretive display at the end of the road explains the story of the Natural Bridge. Bridge Creek flows beneath the ground under the Natural Bridge. Through the centuries, freezing and thawing broke away sections of rock that were carried away by spring runoff, gradually creating the bridge.

There used to be a trail over the bridge, but it was abandoned for fear that the bridge might collapse. Likewise an early proposal to build a road over the bridge was shelved—or you probably wouldn't be able to see it today.

27

ELEPHANT BACK MOUNTAIN

Type of hike: Out-and-back with a little loop at the end.
Total distance: 4 miles or 6.4 kilometers (round-trip).
Elevation gain: 800 feet.
Maps: Trails Illustrated; Yellowstone Lake and Lake USGS Quads.
Starting point: Elephant Back Trailhead.
Finding the trailhead: Drive 0.7 mile south of Fishing Bridge or 0.5 mile north of Lake and park at the small parking area on the west side of the road.

The hike: From some viewpoints this forested ridge looked like an elephant's back to early explorers, but you'll have a hard time getting the same impression when climbing up to the top. Nonetheless it's a nice day hike for anybody staying at Fishing Bridge or Lake, and because of its proximity to these areas, this trail receives heavy use. It also receives heavy maintenance and is in excellent shape and double-wide most of the way.

The trail goes through unburned timber the entire way. About halfway up the hill go left or right on the loop trail. Go either way with no added difficulty and take the other route on the way down. The right fork is the most gradual but longest route to the top, but well-designed switchbacks make the 800-foot climb seem fairly easy whichever fork you choose.

From the viewpoint on top enjoy a panoramic view of "the inland ocean," Yellowstone Lake, and Stevenson Island and the massive Pelican Valley.

Natural Bridge, Elephant Back Mountain

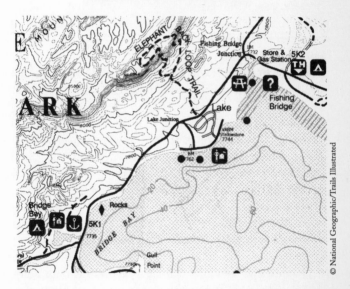

© National Geographic/Trails Illustrated

28
RIDDLE LAKE

Type of hike: Out-and-back.
Total distance: 4.6 miles or 7.4 kilometers (round-trip).
Elevation gain: Minimal.
Maps: Trails Illustrated; Yellowstone Lake and Mount Sheridan USGS Quads.
Starting point: Riddle Lake Trailhead (7K3).
Finding the trailhead: Drive 4.1 miles south of West Thumb and turn into the parking area on the east side of the road.

The hike: This ranks as one of the easiest hikes to a backcountry lake in the park. It's just over 2 miles and flat as a pool table—even though you hike over the Continental Divide!

The trail is in great shape and passes through unburned forest and past several small meadows. Some of the meadows stay marshy until mid-July, so you might get your feet wet—although some of the small stream crossings have foot bridges.

Watch for elk and moose in the meadows—and for bears. The area is a key bear management area, so it remains closed until July 15.

Riddle Lake gets its name because early on in the park's history; it was believed to be a "two-ocean lake" sitting right on the Continental Divide with outlets flowing both east and west. But this was only an early mapping error. The lake is actually about 2 miles east of the Divide where the trailhead is located.

The 274-acre lake also has a large marshy meadow on its southwest corner, and in late summer lilypads float on the surface. Cutthroats swim up Solution Creek from Yellowstone Lake to Riddle Lake.

The trail goes along the north edge of the lake to a small beach where it officially ends. You get a great view of the Red Mountains from the lake.

Riddle Lake

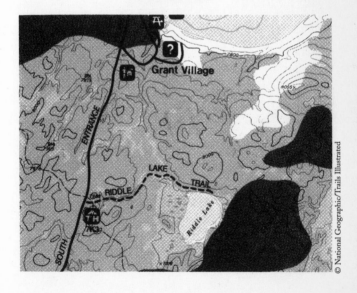

About The Author

In 1979 Bill Schneider, along with his partner, Mike Sample, created Falcon Press Publishing and released two guidebooks the first year. Bill wrote one of them, *Hiking Montana*, which is still a popular guidebook. Since then he has also written eleven more books and many magazine articles on wildlife, outdoor recreation, and environmental issues. Along the way, on a part-time basis over a span of 12 years, Bill has taught classes on bicycling, back-packing, no-trace camping, and hiking in bear country for The Yellowstone Institute, a nonprofit educational organization in Yellowstone National Park. Since 1979 Bill has served as publisher of Falcon Press, which is now established as a premier publisher of recreational guidebooks with more than 350 titles in print.

LEAVE NO TRACE
by Will Harmon

The concept of "leave no trace" seems simple, but it actually gets fairly complicated. This handy quick-reference guidebook includes all the newest information on this growing and all-important subject. The book is written to help the outdoor enthusiast make the hundreds of decisions necessary to protect the natural landscape and still have an enjoyable wilderness experience. Part of the proceeds from the sale of this book go to continue leave-no-trace education efforts.

BEAR AWARE
by Bill Schneider

It's hardly news that Yellowstone is the good habitat for both grizzly and black bears. Hiking in bear country can be very safe if hikers follow the guidelines summarized in this small, "packable" book. Extensively reviewed by bear experts, the book contains the latest information on this intriguing science of bear-human interactions. *Bear Aware* can not only make your hike safer, but it can help you avoid the fear of bears that can take the edge off your trip.

MORE BOOKS ON THE WAY. *Leave No Trace* and *Bear Aware* are two of the first books in a new series of "how to" FalconGuides launched by Falcon Press Publishing in 1997. Coming soon are titles on mountain lion safety, wilderness survival, reading weather, route finding, and other key outdoor skills. All of these quick-reference books are written by experts in the field. In addition, they are "packable" (small enough to fit into a fanny pack) and low-priced.

To order *Leave No Trace* and *Wilderness First Aid* and to find out more about this new series of books, call Falcon at **1-800-582-2665.**

HIKING YELLOWSTONE

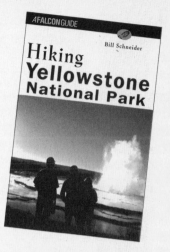

If *Best Easy Day Hikes Yellowstone* whets your appetite for more and perhaps more strenuous hiking in America's first national park, try *Hiking Yellowstone,* a large, comprehensive hiking guidebook by the same author. The hikes in *Best Easy Day Hikes Yellowstone* are also included in *Hiking Yellowstone,* along with 84 more hikes covering 800 miles of trails. The author has taken the immense and complicated trail system and organized it into to logical routes for all types of hikers—all the way from the person who wants a 20-minute self-guided tour to the person who wants a 10-day backpacking adventure.

Hiking Yellowstone is the most comprehensive trail guide to America's first national park, and it does more than just describe the trails. It helps you plan your trip, and it makes it easy to select the hike that's just right for you. It also contains handy trail finder keys, safety information, maps elevation charts, and photos.

Ask for *Hiking Yellowstone* at park visitor centers or order it directly from Falcon by calling **1-800-582-2665.**